IMAGES
of America

BIDDEFORD

Robert H. Gay, one of the principal amateur photographers whose work appears in this book, lived in the old Tristram Morrill house, which was built in 1738. Gay photographed its bull's-eye-glass window. On the sill in the snow is a card with Gay's address. His sense of history and repeated photographic preservations of local scenes has given us a window on the past with a view we could not have hoped for without him. The photograph is from the R.H. Gay Collection, courtesy of the McArthur Library.

IMAGES
of America

BIDDEFORD

Charles L. Butler Jr.

ARCADIA
PUBLISHING

Published by Arcadia Publishing
Charleston, South Carolina

Library of Congress Catalog Card Number: 2003107372

For all general information contact Arcadia Publishing at:
Telephone 843-853-2070
Fax 843-853-0044
E-mail sales@arcadiapublishing.com
For customer service and orders:
Toll-Free 1-888-313-2665

Visit us on the Internet at www.arcadiapublishing.com

The first graphic reference to Biddeford is this map of the Chauacoit (Saco) River, made in 1605 by Samuel de Champlain. Hills Beach is not yet formed, and Biddeford Pool is not enclosed. Fort Hill and the Parker's Neck are islands. Champlain's journal provides evidence that the natives were of Narragansett culture, farming by slash-and-burn methods. Multiple fields are shown along the Saco. The map shows longhouses, wickiups, and palisades. The University of New England in Biddeford now occupies the native village site on the west side. The image is from the McArthur Library.

CONTENTS

ACKNOWLEDGMENTS

The McArthur Library was extremely helpful to me in compiling this book. They gave me access to 1,700 turn-of-the-century photographs. Some of them were taken by professional photographers, but the bulk of them were made by gifted amateurs. Two of these amateurs—Robert H. Gay and Charles Moody—were prolific and deeply interested in genre. Gay was a descendant of Samuel Jordan, founder of one of the oldest families in Biddeford, and he had a deep interest in local history. His family thoughtfully donated his prints and glass negatives to the McArthur Library, greatly enhancing the library's collection. Charles Moody was a Saco resident with the same interests, but he made images of both Biddeford and Saco, Maine. The Moody family donated a number of his prints to the McArthur Library, and many of his glass negatives to the Dyer Library in Saco.

The Biddeford Historical Society allowed me to set up in their office in the McArthur Library and gave me free access to their collection. A number of stereo cards by B.F. Cole have been given to both the society and to the McArthur Library; together they provide an excellent tour of Biddeford's Main Street just after the Civil War.

Someone made all of the photographs used in this book before I was born. Each photographer saw something special that they felt needed to be preserved. They were sufficiently dedicated to its memory to get out the family camera or tripod and make sure the event or item was captured on film. Few of these pictures were published for profit; indeed, most were never seen by others until they were donated to local institutions. Some of the work is not credited, but each image contains something valuable to the history of Biddeford. We owe a debt of gratitude to all of these artists—known and unknown.

INTRODUCTION

Old photographs have always seemed like magic to me. When I was a child, my great-aunt had an old-fashioned stereoscope and a wicker basket full of cards to which I became addicted. My parents bought me a modern 3-D viewer, but it just wasn't the same. Finally, I got an old *Underwood* viewer and some old stereo cards taken in Leadville, Colorado, of real Western types living their daily lives in mud, blood, slosh, and 3-D. When the opportunity to see old photographs in local collections came to me through the Biddeford Historical Society, my enthusiasm was the same. Photographer B.F. Cole was a stereo photographer who made a good record of Biddeford in the 1870s. His images, in particular, caught my attention. When the opportunity arose to assemble some of my favorite photographs to share with others, it was both my pleasure and my challenge.

This book is a collection of old photographs. Portions of Biddeford's story were caught on film and glass plate from 1855 to 1940. I chose the start of the Great Depression as the ending point for this book, as it was a true dividing line in New England history. Little documentation of Biddeford's earliest days survives. Only some old roads, some records, and an old ceramic jug in the Saco Museum remain whole and above ground. The town suffered badly in the struggle for North America between the French and English. Some badly burned artifacts have been unearthed. Every building had been torched during King William's War. Rebuilding began in 1693 with a substantial stone fort, a few houses, and a sawmill. Mills of all types would become the backbone of the town's economy.

Biddeford is an old city by today's standards. It has narrow, crooked streets that town fathers argued over by the square foot. Whose land did it take? How much compensation should they get? The old town records and the records of the First Parish Congregational Church are identical in format. You can see the formation of American democracy take place wherever they hit a snag and acrimonious debate ensues over the mistake. "One man, one vote" and "Don't spend a penny more than you have to" were standard philosophies.

John Oldham and Richard Vines received a grant in 1629 and founded Biddeford. England was moving toward civil war. The Plymouth Company became entangled between king and parliament, and its charter was recalled. The dying company quickly gave out land grants in 1629 to those who had aided it. The colonists arrived on the ship *Swift* and took formal possession on June 25, 1630. Two English planters are known to have been in Biddeford as early as 1628.

John Oldham's name appears first on the grant. He did not involve himself much in the affairs of the town and died at the hands of natives near Block Island in July 1636. They were caught in the act of hiding Oldham's body under a canvas and preparing to sail away with the goods he had hired them to help him trade. Oldham, who was a colorful character, appeared at the Plymouth Colony asking admittance but was a quarrelsome person. Despite Oldham's professions of faith, the leaders of Plymouth never trusted his confessions. Finally, Governor Bradford accused John Oldham of being a spy for the Plymouth Company. He was tried, convicted, and banished from the colony. A record that the ship *Warwick* removed Oldham's goods from Saco to Piscataqua in 1628 possibly indicates a separation of some sort between Oldham and Vines.

Richard Vines was a physician, botanist, soldier, and sailor with a degree from Padua University. This odd combination of talents was just what Fernando Gorges needed when news reached England of a serious epidemic among American Indians. Gorges needed to prove that New England was warm enough for English settlement and that this new disease was not an impediment. The ill-fated Popham Colony blamed failure on Maine's winter weather. Richard Vines and a company of men spent the winter of 1616–1617 at Biddeford Pool and lived among the natives. They were not touched by the plague even as it killed 9 out of 10 of the natives around them. It was likely a European childhood disease, but the symptoms were so severe in the natives that Vines could not diagnose it. When Vines received his grant, he returned to Biddeford Pool, as it was the place he knew best on the Maine coast.

Biddeford became the busiest village in New England in the 1830s. New England's mill fever brought with it the power of heavy investment. The Saco Water Power Company attempted to form Biddeford in the image of Lowell, Massachusetts. Riverside land was bought and power canals were built. The Saco Water Power Company's machine shop was built. Brickyards were opened, and laborers, masons carpenters, machinists, painters, quarrymen, and millwrights were hired and housed in hastily built boardinghouses. The Saco Water Power Company organized other corporations, the first of which was the Laconia Manufacturing Company. When it succeeded, the Pepperell Manufacturing Company was started. Shares for Pepperell sold for $500, and production began in 1850. The stock would split many times and consistently pay a $12-per-share dividend. The Pepperell mills would survive the cotton drought of the Civil War and weave enough Union tent canvas to circle the globe.

One

A NEW NAME FOR
A NEW BEGINNING

Modern Biddeford was a part of Old Saco, a Massachusetts township burned out in 1688. The General Court of Massachusetts appointed a committee to rebuild Maine. Towns completely destroyed were given new names. Cape Porpoise became Arundel, and Saco became Biddeford. Growth was slow until the French were defeated at Louisburg. Then, gains were compounded without destruction and the area prospered from farming, sawmills, gristmills, shipbuilding, and fishing.

This is John Page's plantation at Parker's Neck, Hills Beach, and Biddeford. John Page, a mate on the *Mayflower*, was from Bideford, England. He returned to establish a trading station. Two 17th-century boats similar to the one shown were found at Parker's Neck. The drawing, by Chellis, was made from a James Patterson English print and appeared in *Saco Valley Settlements*, published by Lake Side Press in 1894.

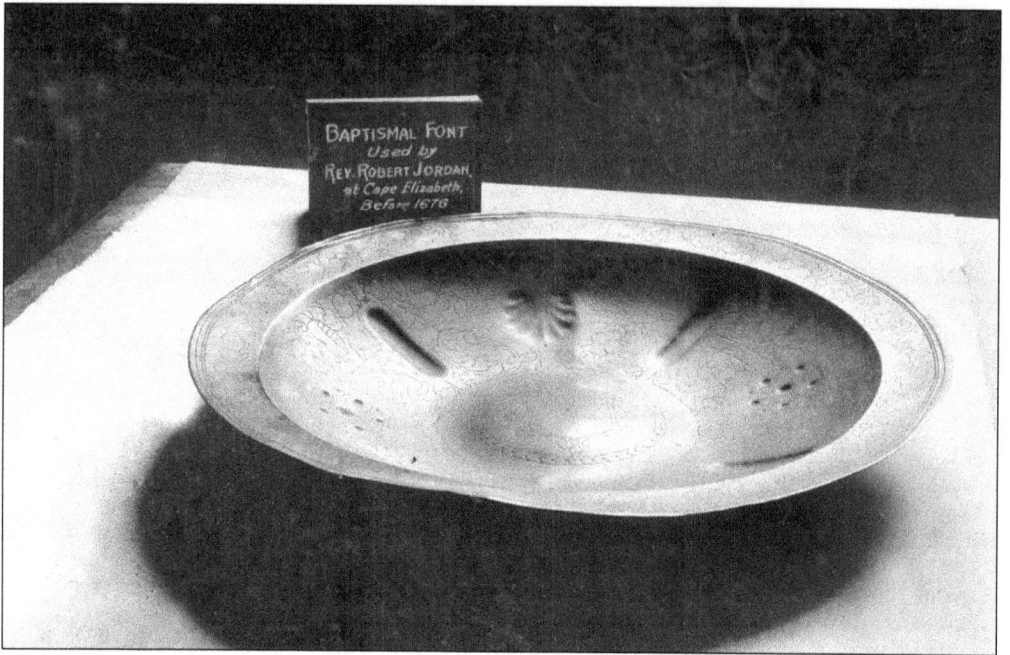

Very few artifacts remain from the earliest settlement of Biddeford or Old Saco. This baptismal font was used by the Reverend Robert Jordan, who acquired most of Cape Elizabeth and lived at Spurwink, splitting his pulpit time between Spurwink and Old Saco. Samuel Jordan, his grandson, would play a key role in establishing the new town of Biddeford. The photograph, from the R.H. Gay Collection, is courtesy of the McArthur Library.

The Samuel Jordan house was built in 1717. The shed to the rear was an American Indian trading post and the only store between Falmouth and York, Maine. Samuel was a prisoner at Three Rivers, Canada, for 13 years. While a prisoner, he learned several native languages. The photograph is courtesy of the Biddeford Historical Society.

10

This is the burial site of Samuel Jordan (1684–1742) in the Jordan burial ground. Jordan was the official interpreter at the 1713 peace talks with American Indians. He was appointed to build a trading post when the natives requested it. He built it and his home a few hundred feet from the site of John Page's plantation.

The Benjamin Haley house, built c. 1718, is currently the oldest house in Biddeford. Haley acquired the land in Biddeford when he was an painter's apprentice for his uncle in Boston. He returned and built the new town of Biddeford Meetinghouse. He built and kept a ferry at the Old Town Landing. The photograph is from the R.H. Gay Collection, courtesy of the McArthur Library.

This bronze plaque was placed near the site of the Benjamin Haley meetinghouse by the Daughters of the American Revolution in 1904. It is located at the intersection of New Town Road and Sokokis Road. Benjamin Haley kept a ferry on the Saco River near this stone. The Old Town Burial Ground is also located here. This photograph is from the R.H. Gay Collection, courtesy of the McArthur Library.

This monument was also erected by the Daughters of the American Revolution. It marks the site of Fort Mary, the scene of several colonists' deaths at the hands of the French and American Indians. To the left in the distance is the Jordan trading post of 1717, and the land in the background is Parker's Neck. Fort Mary was completed c. 1710. This photograph is from the R.H. Gay Collection, courtesy of the McArthur Library.

This is the home of Judge Rishworth Jordan, the eldest son of Samuel Jordan. Rishworth was born in 1719 in the old trading post and died in 1808. This house was built *c.* 1745 on the site of a 1720 garrison on the hill that is now part of the University of New England campus. His descendants lived in and added to the old house for more than 100 years. The house is now Stella Maris Hall. The photograph is courtesy of the McArthur Library.

The First Parish Meetinghouse of Biddeford was built in 1759 to replace the Haley meetinghouse. Dispute over the location resulted in the separation of Saco from Biddeford, as residents on the eastern side were tired of 40 years of ferry crossings. The building was remodeled in 1840 in the Greek Revival style and was the political and religious center of Biddeford. The photograph is courtesy of the Biddeford Historical Society.

This view shows the interior of the First Parish Church in 1893. The carpet and hanging lamps date from 1840. The pews date from 1759, when the building was constructed. The pump organ was donated in 1893. The Empire-style furniture is upholstered in horsehair, and the pew seats are stuffed with horsehair. The photograph is courtesy of the Biddeford Historical Society.

This house was the home of Jeremiah Hill and Samuel Pierson. It is situated midway on Pierson's Lane. Jeremiah Hill was at Harvard in 1775, when the port of Boston was closed. He organized a company of men to go to Boston and fight for the liberation of the city. After the war, he was tried for heresy in the First Parish Church. The photograph is by Charles E. Moody, courtesy of the McArthur Library.

Samuel Pierson, born in Boston, saw a victim of the Boston Massacre die on his parents' doorstep. He joined the Revolution in 1776 at the age of 17. Because of his youth, he was made George Washington's clerk at the battle of Boston. He helped establish the Unitarian church in Portland after the war and came to Biddeford to work in the area's first bank in 1792. He became Jeremiah Hill's son-in-law and later purchased the Hill house on Pierson's Lane. He started the tradition of "Tar Tub Day," the celebration of Washington's Birthday with bonfires in Biddeford. The image is from the collection of the Saco Museum–Dyer Library, in Saco, Maine.

The Tristram Morrell house, built in 1738 on Decary Road, was the home of R.H. Gay, who took many of these photographs. The fruit peddler is Simon Epstein, whose shop was in Old Orchard. The photograph is from the R.H. Gay Collection, courtesy of the McArthur Library.

The Capt. Nathaniel Hill Felker house was the only home on the Pool Road lost in the 1947 forest fire. Felker (born in 1821) was the son of John and Sarah (Gilpratrick) Felker. He went to sea at the age of nine. He had his master's papers at the age of 19 and was the master of vessels for more than 50 years, never losing a ship or a single sailor. The photograph, a gift of J. Vaughan Dennet, is courtesy of the McArthur Library.

Captain Felker's sister Sarah married Joseph Gray Johnson. The Johnsons and Felkers held a reunion in 1882. Seated in the center are Mary, Martha, Susannah, and Sarah Felker. To the right of them is Capt. Nathaniel Felker (wearing a felt hat). The barefoot boy with a vest (in the front on the right) is the author's great-grandfather Charles A. Johnson. The photograph is from the author's collection.

Wood Island Light, at Biddeford Pool, was built in 1808 of local stone. This photograph was made c. 1875. The keeper's home was rebuilt in 1869 with Victorian details. The pyramid building on the left housed the fog sounding machinery. Despite the lighthouse, several ships were lost on local rocks and beaches. The photograph is courtesy of the McArthur Library.

17

Photographer Baldwin Coolidge of Boston visited Biddeford *c.* 1883. He sold many contact prints of his work and helped illustrate Joseph W. Smith's *Gleanings from the Sea.* He caught these old salts doing the unpleasant but time-honored job of splitting fish. Fishing supported Biddeford coastal families for generations. The photograph is courtesy of the McArthur Library.

Biddeford Falls Village had built up around the shipyard on Water Street in the early 1800s. This is the home of James Sullivan, a delegate to the Continental Congress, governor of Massachusetts in 1807, and author of the first history of Maine. He built this house in 1770 and added the front in 1774. The photograph is by Charles E. Moody, courtesy of the McArthur Library.

Seth Spring, one of the members of Jeremiah Hill's 1775 Militia Company, returned to Biddeford with Moses Bradbury, another war veteran. They developed Springs Island and were the first to use the Saco River to power mills. This building was the Bell and Bridge Tavern, built by Seth Spring in 1798. The photograph, taken c. 1890, is courtesy of the McArthur Library.

America was forced to fight a second war of independence in 1812. Biddeford had its own star-spangled banner. Some 150 British soldiers invaded Biddeford Pool. The old trading post was fortified, and Capt. Waldo Hill flew this flag over the old trading post and on his ship. The flag is now in the Smithsonian. The photograph is courtesy of the McArthur Library.

The bones of the destroyed ship *Equator* can be seen running left to center of this picture. Some 150 British Marines raised havoc with Colonel Cutts' holdings at Biddeford Pool in the War of 1812. The fact that he was President Madison's brother-in-law made him an attractive target. This photograph was made *c.* 1887 and is courtesy of the Biddeford Historical Society.

This navigation monument was erected in 1825 on Stage Island to mark the entrance to the harbor for tacking sailing ships. The first monument collapsed, killing the contractor. His wife and a new crew completed this monument with a second government appropriation. The photograph is courtesy of the McArthur Library.

Judge George Thatcher is shown here in a photograph of an 1820 painting by Henry Williams. Thatcher was influential in the separation of Maine from Massachusetts. He was born in 1754, elected to Congress in 1787, and served 14 years before resigning to serve in the Massachusetts Supreme Court. He died in Biddeford in 1824. The photograph is courtesy of the McArthur Library.

Judge Thatcher, Harvard class of 1776, was a delegate from Massachusetts to the Continental Congress. His small home on South Street housed Biddeford's best library in the 1820s. He was representative from the district of Maine and cast the first abolitionist vote in Congress in 1800. The photograph is courtesy of the McArthur Library.

This Federal house is typical of those on the Biddeford Heights above Water Street. Unfortunately, they have been vastly altered from their original appearance by years of repair and subdivision. This is the James Maxwell House, on High Street. The photograph is by Charles E. Moody, courtesy of the McArthur Library.

Located on the corner of Hill and Main Streets, this is the home of Dr. Horace Bacon. The doctor began practice here in 1826 and continued until his death in 1888 at the age of 84. These Federal buildings are now altered with storefronts. The photograph is by Charles E. Moody, courtesy of the McArthur Library.

Unitarianism was popular among war veterans; it made for stirrings in the church. Jeremiah Hill was tried in the First Parish Church for heresy. He and others formed the Second Religious Society and built a church in 1797 on South Street. This Victorian building is on the same site, a remodeling of the congregation's second building done in 1870. The photograph is courtesy of the McArthur Library.

Methodism spread rapidly through Biddeford in the 1800s. Many First Parish Congregational families joined the South Biddeford Methodist Church, built in 1836. A church was built in town in 1847 on Alfred Street and another at Oak Ridge in 1853. Eventually there would be five Methodist churches; today there are none. The photograph is courtesy of the Biddeford Historical Society.

Farming was the same for scores of years; the dairy and hayfield were the center of it. These hay forkers in Biddeford in 1905 are as scarce now as working farms. The workers slaked their thirst with molasses- and ginger-flavored water to wash down the chaff and dust. They always seemed to be forced into a race with a thunderstorm for the crop. The photograph is courtesy of the Biddeford Historical Society.

The lumber industry was well established in colonial times. These men are freeing up logs stranded by low water on the Saco River in the 1920s. On wider, calmer parts of the river, the logs were constrained in rafts and booms. The river was a constant hazard, not only for loggers but for daredevil children attracted by the booms. The photograph is courtesy of the McArthur Library.

24

This is a photograph of a painting by an unknown artist in Canton Harbor. The *Mount Washington* was the largest clipper ship built in Biddeford. Built at the height of the China trade, it weighed 1,217 tons, had a 37-foot beam, and was 184 feet long. The cost of this ship in 1867 was $110,000. The photograph is courtesy of the McArthur Library.

Capt. Rishworth Jordan used this house only when ashore. His cousin Tristram Morrell built the house in 1738. His grandson R.H. Gay lived here as well. It is a tribute to first-growth pine; nobody remembers any paint on the place for the last 265 years. The home is typical of the older homes along the Saco River, joined to small barns by a long shed. The photograph, from the R.H. Gay Collection, is courtesy of the McArthur Library.

The Lassell-Ward house marks the eastern end of the Old King's Highway in Biddeford. The ferry to Saco was here except for four years when Benjamin Haley kept it at the Old Town Landing. The house is on the National Register of Historic Places because of the paneling on its walls and ceilings. The photograph is courtesy of the Biddeford Historical Society, a gift of the Ward family.

The Edwards Cottage was known as the Whale Bone Cottage because of Mr. Edwards's front gate made of whale jaws. The cottage was built in 1875 but retains Greek Revival details. The ornate shingles reveal its Victorian origins. This land was the home of Richard Hitchcock, one of Biddeford's early settlers. The photograph is courtesy of the McArthur Library.

Two

A Mechanized
Way of Life

One Biddeford family who lived at Kings Corner in 1820 always rose at dawn. They placed their rooster on a roost inside the fireplace (in case he made droppings) so that at first light he would crow and wake the family. The Industrial Revolution would change things considerably. Biddeford became known as "the City of Bells," with clock bells regulating every part of daily life. Factory bells, rules, and wages regulated all activity.

Some 12 million bricks were used in the construction of the Laconia Mills. Workers needed housing, so four boardinghouses like those on the left and right were built to house them. This view is at the end of York Street, looking through the court of the boardinghouses to the main entrance of Laconia Mill No. 2. Production began in 1845. The photograph, a gift of Prescott Howard, is from the McArthur Library.

Samuel Batchelder, born in 1784, transformed Biddeford from a village to a city. He had a vision of a textile manufacturing center and a city. He was a director of the mills in Saco, Maine, in 1831 and realized that Biddeford was better suited for waterpower than Saco. Batchelder had developed the Hamilton Mills in Lowell and had been called in as an advisor in Saco. He developed the Saco Water Power Company in 1837 to prepare mill privileges and build mills. He incorporated the Laconia Mills in 1841 and the Pepperell Mills in 1844. The image is from the McArthur Library.

The first building erected was the Saco Water Power Company machine shop, shown on the left side of the river. Built in 1841, the shop produced cotton textile machinery for the Laconia and Pepperell Mills, then machines for export. The photograph is from the McArthur Library.

The Saco River is capable of producing some severe flooding. This 1895 view shows why water-powered mills had to be built so rugged. The foundations and walls had to consist of many feet of masonry materials to withstand forces like this. The feed and waste of the turbines was through 27-foot-diameter tunnels. A depth of over 30 feet was needed for them. The photograph is courtesy of the McArthur Library.

William P. Hanes was a graduate of Dartmouth College. He taught school for a short time. He then came to Saco to read law under Governor Fairfield and was trusted with the firm when the governor was away. He became land agent for the Saco Water Power Company and acquired a large tract of land on Adams Street. He built a mansion in the midst of a large garden there after he became agent of the Pepperell Mills and later company treasurer. His chief claim to fame was his deft handling of the Civil War cotton drought and keeping the Pepperell Mills in production through the war. The image is courtesy of the Biddeford Historical Society.

When work on the Pepperell Mills began, labor was scarce and help was recruited from Canada. Israel Shevenell worked in the brickyards of Biddeford when he was 19 years old. He made the trip in 1845 through 18 inches of spring mud (his small dog died from the effort). He was the first to come from French Canada and stay; he became a U.S. citizen in 1865. The photograph is from the McArthur Library.

This view shows Moise Cartier, who also came to Biddeford to make brick. Unlike Israel Shevenell, he stuck to that job for years and was working at the Saco brickyard in 1900. English speakers nicknamed him Moses Quarter. He was known to throw a raw brick to children so that they might play with the clay. He died in Saco in 1924 at the age of 93. The photograph is courtesy of the McArthur Library.

This is an 1855 photograph of the Biddeford House, on City Square in Biddeford. The hotel was built by the Saco Water Power Company in 1847. With 100 rooms, it was the largest hotel north of Boston. John C. Robbins, a respected Portland innkeeper who was recruited for the new hotel, advertised on the portico. Few pictures of the portico exist. The photograph is courtesy of the McArthur Library.

Biddeford High School was built to meet the demands for better-educated workers in 1847–1848 and was in the same style as the Biddeford House. The school bell served as the town's first fire alarm. The fire company was formed nearby. The photograph is courtesy of the Biddeford Historical Society.

The high school became the Washington Street Grammar School by 1907. The blackboard is decorated for February 26, 1907. Patterned wallpaper in a public building is unusual. The statue in the corner appears to be Athena, the Greek goddess of wisdom. The photograph is courtesy of the McArthur Library, a gift of Lena Holt Fraser.

These boardinghouses were erected for the Pepperell Mills in 1848. They were in the same style as the Biddeford House and Biddeford High School. Women in boardinghouses like these were the first source of labor unrest because of excessive paternalism in the boardinghouse rules. The photograph is courtesy of the McArthur Library.

The management of the Pepperell Mills gathered outside the Pepperell Counting House in 1895, a time when the success of the mill was approaching its zenith. The upper room of this building was used over the years as a Catholic church, an Abolitionist's Congregational church, and a mosque. The mills made Biddeford streets a babble by recruiting labor from around the world. The photograph is courtesy of the McArthur Library.

This is an early spinning room in the Pepperell Mills. The large bobbins indicate it was a second spinning. Note the skirted longhaired woman peeking out of a maze of belts and pulleys. The unguarded whirling belts and bobbins liked to grab things, and more than one worker was scalped or flung from floor to ceiling. This photograph, from the R.H. Gay Collection, is courtesy of the McArthur Library.

Spinning mules are seen in the Pepperell Mills in 1907. In the early years of textile machines, they were the only way to spin fine strong thread. Mule spinners were skilled workers. When new, less complicated spinning machines were invented, mule spinners were laid off or transferred to lower-paying jobs. The photograph is from the R.H. Gay Collection, courtesy of the McArthur Library.

This is the engine room of the Pepperell Mills in 1907. Steam and, later, electricity were more dependable power sources than water. The annual run of eels could cause the turbines to fail. Every summer, eels stopped all production with a grizzly tangled mess. Crews had to spear eels in the turbine intake grills to make things spin again. This photograph is from the R.H. Gay Collection, courtesy of the McArthur Library.

Carding was the first step in cloth production. This is a carding room in 1910. It produced a fat, loose rope of cotton with the fibers all arranged along its length. Different techniques of drawing and spinning could change this into several different weights and strengths of thread. The photograph is from the R.H. Gay Collection, courtesy of the McArthur Library.

This is a spinning room in 1910. Spinning had to be done several times; each time, the thread would become longer and more tightly wound. Doffers were employed to continuously change the spinning bobbins. The blur on the left is a busy doffer among hundreds of bobbins. The photograph is from the R.H. Gay Collection, courtesy of the McArthur Library.

This is a web drawing room 1910. Hundreds of threads on the racks at the left were wound parallel to each other on the large bobbin on the right called a "beam." The beam would be placed on the back of a loom and provide the web of the cloth after the tedious business of harness picking. The photograph is from the R.H. Gay Collection, courtesy of the McArthur Library.

This is a good view of the front of a draper loom in the Pepperell Mills c. 1910. Thread for the shuttle is stored in the cylinders on the right of the machine. Weavers were notoriously tone deaf from the clack of the shuttle. A special mode of speech had to be adopted so they could hear one another. The photograph is from the R.H. Gay Collection, courtesy of the McArthur Library.

This is an early cloth hall in one of Biddeford's mills, where the women appear to be dressed in a c. 1890 style. The cloth in the foreground shows the type of flaw that had to be removed. The workers removed sections of cloth with bad threads and stains. Sections of full yardage were pressed and bundled at the end of the room. The photograph is courtesy of the Biddeford Historical Society.

Pictured in 1907 is a cloth hall in the Pepperell Mills. The inspection is done by machine, and the room has electric lights. Automatic knives triggered by foot pedals cut out the flaws, but the workers still scrub, bleach, and pick flaws in the cloth. The room is surprisingly light and pleasant. The photograph is courtesy of the McArthur Library.

Three

GILDED AGE MAIN STREET

Biddeford was hit hard by the Civil War. At one time, two-thirds of the mills were closed because of the lack of cotton. The most able-bodied men served in the war. Progress was rapid when the flow of cotton returned. The industrial engine began to produce a cornucopia of goods, and by 1880, the city was changing as Main Street acquired a row of large brick stores filled with goods nobody ever imagined would be available.

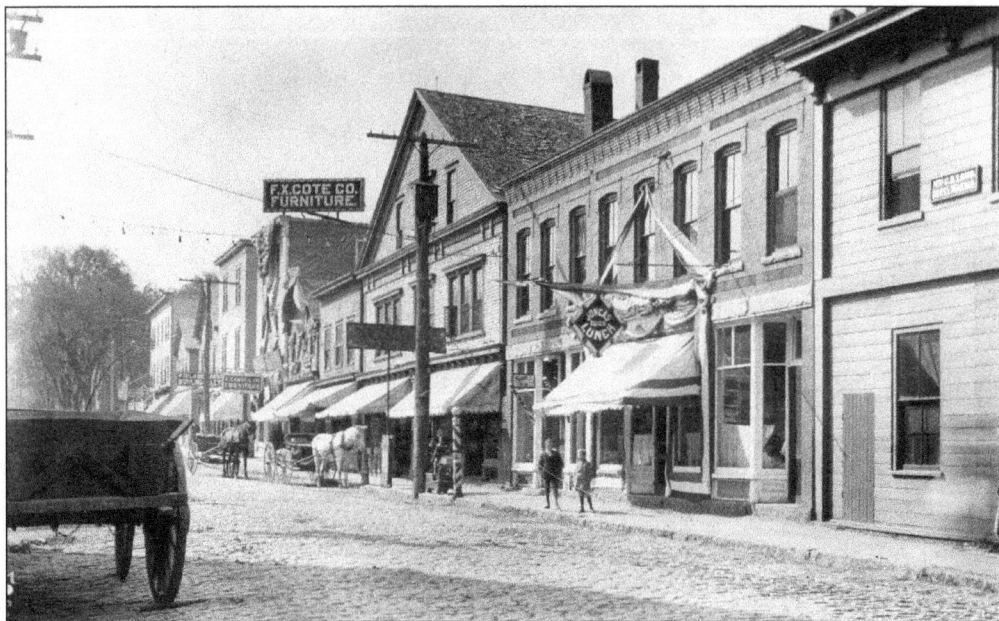

This is Washington Street in 1909. The building with the gable roof is the Somes Building. Built in 1854, it was originally on the corner of Washington and Main Streets. It was used as Biddeford's first city hall from 1855 to 1860. Daniel Somes, the first mayor of the city, built it. The photograph is from the R.H. Gay Collection, courtesy of the McArthur Library.

This is Daniel Somes, born in Laconia, New Hampshire, in 1815. He came to Biddeford to print the *Eastern Journal* in 1846. He sold the paper and prospered at other occupations, including manufacturing loom harnesses, making paint and varnishes, opening the First National Bank, and beginning Biddeford's mass production of shoes. He was elected to Congress in 1858. He served well but resigned his seat in March 1861 to sit on the Peace Commission, which tried desperately to avert the Civil War. He then worked as a patent attorney until his death in 1888. The photograph is courtesy of the McArthur Library.

Somes developed Somesville in Saco and made it a success by building the Somesville Bridge. It put rural Saco in reach of the factories in the heart of both cities and made the area prime housing lots. The photograph is courtesy of the McArthur Library.

B.F. Cole took several stereographs of Main Street in 1872, just seven years after the end of the Civil War. Biddeford's growth was detoured briefly by the war. This view is of the bridge to Saco at Liberty Square at the south end of Main Street. These bridges were universally hated for spooking horses and were replaced in 1877. The photograph is courtesy of the McArthur Library.

This Cole view is north of the first and looks south. It shows the intersection of Main and Alfred Streets. The Greek Revival store block on the right is Hill's Block. The south corner of Alfred Street is filled with Francis Meed's grocery store. The photograph is courtesy of the McArthur Library.

Taken in 1870, this Cole stereo is looking north from Alfred Street. The long striped poles are barber poles. The unsightly shed roofs over the sidewalks protected goods from the sun and protected pedestrians from falling snow or rain. Only the crosswalks are paved with stone; the street is dirt, mud, and horse droppings. The steeple at the center is the Pavilion Church. The photograph is courtesy of the McArthur Library.

Here the scene is looking from Jefferson Street to City Square. The building on the left housed McKenney's Ambrotype Studio. The Biddeford House (with its original portico) is shown, as is the 1860 city hall and opera house. The Sweetser Building can be seen on the right. The photograph is courtesy of the McArthur Library, a gift of Mrs. C.R. Means.

Biddeford City Hall and opera house were built in 1860 to replace the Central Block, which burned in 1858. The new city building had stores on the first floor to replace the business locations lost when the Central Block burned. The new opera house opened in October 1860 with the Civil War–era play *The Octoroon*. The photograph, likely by B.F. Cole, is courtesy of the McArthur Library.

This photograph shows the whole front of the Sweetser Block on Main Street. The hitching posts on the left are for city hall patrons. The building was made of wood but was painted a light and dark tan to imitate sandstone. The *Biddeford Daily Journal* was published here for several years. Fleet Bank now occupies the site. The photograph is courtesy of the McArthur Library.

City Square is shown in 1870 from the roof of the 1860 city hall. The Biddeford House is on the right. The Pepperell Counting House is on the left. The Crystal Arcade is in the center. The background shows Laconia Mill No. 2, as well as three of the Laconia boardinghouses. The photograph is courtesy of the McArthur Library.

This is North Main Street. In 1868, it was called Chestnut Street. It was built by the Saco Water Power Company by blowing away the side of Ram-Cat Hill while building a road to the Portsmouth and Portland Railroad depot. Train service began in 1842. The work was done before the Laconia Mills were built in 1844. The photograph, a gift of Carlton Foss, is courtesy of the McArthur Library.

This is how B.F. Cole saw upper Main Street looking south from Jefferson Street in 1875. The first building housed the Union and Journal before it moved to the Sweetser Block. The lot is currently the Biddeford Savings Bank. The small square building is Reilly's Bakery, and the gable-roofed building is Bert's Barber Shop. Everything shown here is now gone. The photograph is courtesy of the McArthur Library.

The Pavilion Church was built in 1863 by abolitionists displeased with the Second Parish Church's position on slavery. It was named after a pavilion tent erected on the lawn of the Second Parish by those not willing to worship there. John Stevens, who designed the First Parish Church of Saco, designed the church. This brick building with Victorian ornament was the finest Protestant church building in the city despite the Civil War economy. The photograph, courtesy of the McArthur Library, is a gift of Ruth Hussy.

46

The sanctuary of the Pavilion Church had plenty of heavy Victorian plaster molding, but most of it in this photograph is faux painting. Interior painting of this type was popular in Maine in the Victorian period. Much of it throughout the state has been lost because it was not real fresco painting and has chipped off the plaster. The photograph is from the McArthur Library.

Across the street from the Pavilion Church was the Warren Block, built by Dr. Francis G. Warren in 1870. He had a large home and office on Elm Street just outside the photograph on the right. The Warren Block was the first brick business block on upper Main Street. The photograph is by B.F. Cole, courtesy of the McArthur Library.

You did not have it made in the 1880s until your name was on a new masonry business block. Orin H. Staples hired architect Charles Kimball of Portland to design his. The initials *O.H.S.* appear in the cornice, and a large *S* flag flies above the store roof. The brick was sheathed in highly visible white marble. The top floor was the Palestine Masonic Lodge; the second floor was filled with business offices. The store on the first floor made the first use of plate glass in Biddeford. The photograph is from the McArthur Library.

The *Biddeford Daily Journal* was in the Sweetser Block from 1891 to 1905, when it moved to a building on Adams Street. Billboards on each side of the door advertise the paper by posting the latest news. The Sweetser building was several storefronts long; its piecemeal loss did not improve Main Street. The site is on the corner of Main and Lincoln Streets. The photograph is courtesy of the McArthur Library.

The *Biddeford Daily Journal* got architect John Calvin Stevens of Portland to design a new building for them on Adams Street in 1906. The building has massive beams to hold the press and paper .The French paper *La Justice* and the telephone company were tenants. The photograph, a gift of Miriam Hayford Small, is courtesy of the McArthur Library.

The interior of Tom Evans's department store on Main Street in 1899 was filled with goods. Gaslights are in use even though electric power is available. Unlike in today's self-service stores, the goods here were separated from the customer, as in a jewelry store. Every purchase required the help of a clerk. The photograph is courtesy of the McArthur Library.

Millinery stores were popular. Hat making was considered an art like flower arraigning. Ornament meant wealth. Twentieth-century dress would become plainer and cheaper. Most women could only afford one or two items from a fancy goods store like this and had to adorn their dresses with tatting or crochet work made at home. The photograph is courtesy of the Biddeford Historical Society.

Four

A BALANCE OF
REWARD AND EVILS

In the mid-1800s, unfettered capitalism produced "swollen fortunes" for those with corporate power. It also produced enough wealth to allow the government to attempt social change for the general welfare of the people. Public schools and public health and labor laws improved the common man's lot. Science produced solutions to the crowding and sickness caused by city life.

The care of the sick and elderly began to be a problem as early as 1820. Care of Biddeford's poor and sick citizens was "auctioned off" to the lowest bidder at town meetings. The city poor farm was established to stop the resulting injustices. The first act of city government was to purchase the Dominicus Cut's Farm as a home for the aged and indigent. The photograph is courtesy of the Biddeford Historical Society.

The home of the most important citizen of Biddeford was the Pepperell Manufacturing Company's agent's house, at the corner of Adams and Jefferson Streets. Originally built by the Saco Water Power Company in the Greek Revival style, it was modernized by the addition of Italianate details when sold to Pepperell. The photograph, taken by Merner Staebler in 1911, is from a postcard in the author's collection.

The Gould House, near the intersection of Alfred and Birch Streets, was the first brick building on Alfred Street. It was built in 1829 just after the first mills in Saco were erected. Mr. Gould was criticized for moving so far out of town at the time. His son would be able to operate a profitable store on the corner of Birch and Alfred in just a few years. The photograph is courtesy of the McArthur Library.

Judge Samuel Luques studied law at Harvard. His family originated in Paris, France. He moved to Biddeford and set up a law practice 1846. He then served on the school board and the municipal court starting in 1879. He acquired a great many rental properties and became a wealthy landlord to many mill workers. The photograph is courtesy of the McArthur Library.

Simon Newcomb built this mansion in the wedge between South and Crescent Streets. He was the leading shoe manufacturer in Biddeford. The lawn of this home now contains Christ Episcopal Church and a flooring shop. The large home behind it is the home of N.C. Cole. The photograph is courtesy of the McArthur Library.

The Means House, on South Street, was built in 1850 near the end of the Greek Revival period. The Pepperell Mills started production the same year. The columns are copies of classical Ionic order, because Americans associated their republic with ancient Greece. This was first indigenous style of American architecture. The photograph is courtesy of the McArthur Library, a gift of C.R. Means.

The home of Jonathan Tuck is on the corner of Jefferson and Adams Streets. Jonathan was Biddeford's postmaster and second mayor. He died in office in 1861. The home has a mix of Greek and Italian Renaissance details. The brackets are typical of the transition in styles. The photograph is courtesy of the McArthur Library.

Timothy Shaw was in business his whole life. He started clerking in is father's Sanford store at the age of nine. He was born in 1783 and came to Biddeford in 1865 to be treasurer of the Shaw & Clark Sewing Machine Company. He was later city assessor for Biddeford. The photograph is courtesy of the Biddeford Historical Society.

New utilities appeared in the 1880s. The telephone company was at 156 Main Street. The exchange began with only 35 telephones. Those shown are, from left to right, Thomas Quint (lineman), Frank Goodwin, Dean Tolman (manager), Mrs. Luther Day, Zora Seavey (bookkeeper), Mrs. Walter Robbins, Mary Aitken, Mrs. Ned Chadbourne, and Mrs. Abraham Kay. The photograph is courtesy of the McArthur Library.

Charles Hardey built this home on Adams Street. He came to Biddeford in 1845 to be an overseer in the Laconia Mills; he later became general overseer of the Pepperell Mills. He invented the Hardy Card Grinder in 1851 and purchased the rights to several English textile inventions. He manufactured them in the Hardy Machine Company, formed in 1866. The photograph is courtesy of the Biddeford Historical Society.

The cliché "I told Tom Edison it wouldn't work" might apply here, but two deaths preclude any humor. History repeated itself, because an earlier plant on Main Street in Saco blew up in the same fashion in 1899. Service had begun in 1888. The explosion leveled the Biddeford electric station on September 3, 1900. Power was knocked out in Biddeford, Saco, and Old Orchard. The photograph is courtesy of the McArthur Library.

When York Heat and Light was not blowing up, it could put on a novel display. The streets were decorated with lights for a merchants' carnival in 1906. The diamond-shaped business signs were a stock item, and several businesses had them. The higher lights in the distance are on Biddeford City Hall. The photograph is from the R.H. Gay Collection, courtesy of the McArthur Library.

Stable power generation to the area came with the York Heat and Light Company's plant on Water Street. The plant was built in 1907. Electric power was slow to come into general use. It was not until the 1920s that it was cheap enough for the average person to use. Then, the families who used it carefully rationed it. The photograph, courtesy of the McArthur Library, is from the R.H. Gay Collection.

Biddeford got its water from wells and cisterns and had no sewer system. The population got denser, and Biddeford had the dubious distinction of having the highest death rate from infectious disease in Maine. The Biddeford-Saco Water Company was chartered in 1880. A reservoir on a nearby hill supplied Biddeford, Saco, and Old Orchard by gravity feed in 1885. The photograph is courtesy of the McArthur Library.

Treated water did not go down Pool Street until 1928. It was brought to Biddeford Pool from Goose Rocks Beach in 1915. The schooner in the gut is carrying a load of water pipe for the system. The children are Phyllis and Mary Means. The beach was not a residential area before the arrival of fresh water. The photograph is from the R.H. Gay Collection, courtesy of the McArthur Library.

Student health problems prompted the building of Birch Street School in 1880. Typhoid fever had emptied the Foss Street School. Architect Charles Kimball of Portland chose wood as his medium and put the savings into the interior. It had central heat ventilation and soundproof floors. The location high above the city was thought healthful, as well. The photograph is courtesy of the McArthur Library.

This is a room of the Birch Street School. Interior woodwork was black walnut with ash floors. The windows had black walnut shutters instead of curtains. Metal ventilators connected with the roof to prevent low humidity, and ceilings were high to prevent lung disease. The photograph is courtesy of the McArthur Library.

Built near the Birch Street School on the hill above the city in 1887, St. Joseph's Grammar School was high style, the finest school in the city. It set a parochial school standard that the public school system was hard pressed to match. It was larger and better designed than any city school. The image is courtesy of the McArthur Library and is from a church pamphlet.

Parochial schools were a blessing to children of parents who were often illiterate in both French and English. Unfortunately, the schools did little to relieve the insularity of the French-speaking community. Assimilation into American culture was avoided for several generations. These students are posing outside of St. Joseph's School. The photograph is courtesy of the McArthur Library.

Biddeford organized its school districts and rebuilt its rural schools in the 1860s. The Morrell School was built on Smith farmland in 1860. It was named for Reverend Morrell, Biddeford's minister through the French and Indian War and the American Revolution. It is now a private residence on Decary Road. The photograph is from the author's collection.

The school district at Biddeford Pool was No. 8. The children are posing outside in 1882. The site is that of the current firehouse. The well-dressed boy wearing a Civil War kepi is Thomas L. Evans. The Civil War kepi was a favorite hat for boys until 1900. The photograph is courtesy of the McArthur Library.

The Washington Street High School was replaced in 1890 by this building on Alfred Street. The striking design is by Charles Wadlin, who also designed the Thornton Academy building in Saco. The building is wonderful in form and now enjoys a second life as a cultural center. The photograph is courtesy of the McArthur Library.

These well-dressed citizens were the night school staff of the Biddeford Evening School in 1900. Night school operation proved necessary to improve adult education and to promote English and citizenship for many newcomers. Greek, Italian, Gaelic, Farsi, and French made quite a mix on the streets in 1900. The photograph is courtesy of the McArthur Library.

A public sewer system was sorely needed. Knowledge of the terrain and cost postponed its construction until 1911. Ponds of standing septic on the plains beyond Birch Street prompted the building. This is the sewer excavation in front of city hall. Rock was so hard that a steam-powered jackhammer had to be used. The Otto Nelson Company of Bangor was the contractor. Near the steam drill is Ray Wakefield. Next to him is Lewis Richardson. Above them on the platform are Officer George Fry and John Beatty of Bangor. In front are the project civil engineer, John Talon, and Edward Gagnon, with an iron bar. The photograph is from the R.H. Gay Collection, courtesy of the McArthur Library.

When the sewer system was under construction, Jeffery Hartwell and Charles Lowell boarded with the Johnsons on Summer Street. Mr. Johnson was trimming the interior of Thomas Emery School. Hartwell and Lowell worked for the Otto Nelson Company in 1913. Putting up with the mud was worth the board. The photograph is from the author's collection.

This is not snow on Main Street in 1914, but dirt from sewer work. Before the sewer was installed, men with "honey carts" removed night soil while others slept. Cesspools could actually leak into a neighbor's basement. For the thousands in Biddeford, it was a distinct health risk. The photograph is from the R.H. Gay Collection, courtesy of the McArthur Library.

The new Thomas Emery Union School shows behind these curious digging machines. Biddeford was in the middle of installing public sewers in 1912. The gasoline engine on the trailer powered the derrick drop hammer. The trolley tracks in the foreground are those of the Atlantic Shore Line Interurban System. The photograph is from the author's collection.

This is Miss Staple's class at Thomas Emery Union School on January 1, 1916. The interior of the new school had hard maple floors and woodwork. All rooms were ventilated. Intercoms connected classrooms to the office. The photograph is from the author's collection.

Five

THE HIGHER ARTS

Biddeford was known as a good show town. It was the third stop on the summer stock road out of Boston. The town had much local talent that was recognized throughout the region. When a new hospital was needed, the local hospital association was able to raise thousands of dollars by putting on shows.

The Gilbert and Sullivan Company gave several performances and thought to have their costumes and sets photographed. This is the cast of *Pirates of Penzance*. The stage setting is suggestive of the Modern Major General's sleepwalking scene. The photograph is courtesy of the Biddeford Historical Society.

Ella Johnson, born in 1856, was the individual who profited most from the musical atmosphere in 19th century in Biddeford. She was the youngest child of Joseph Gray Johnson and Sarah (Felker) Johnson. She began as a song demonstrator in John C. Hanes's music store in Biddeford, eventually partnering with him in the music publishing business. They eventually had offices in San Francisco, Chicago, Boston, and Washington, D.C. Johnson invested her profits in Bell Telephone, and on Christmas 1932, she gave $1,000 checks to her 20-plus nephews. After five years of economic depression, it was a generous gift. The photograph is by W. Bell of Washington, D.C., and is from the author's collection.

Pierre Painchaud was the most talented of 19th-century Biddeford musicians. He was born in Walton, Canada, in 1852. He was the grandson of Anna Matthews, the only female member of the London Symphony. He learned music through self-study. He had a snappy personal flair that Victorian Americans loved. He was also a quick-change artist and a character actor. His La Fanfare Painchaud became recognized as the best band in New England. He also started a French theater company and a Philharmonic Orchestra. The photograph is courtesy of the Biddeford Historical Society.

Pierre Painchaud started his own band in 1870 at the age of 18. This is an early picture of the band taken in 1872 before they had uniforms. Their early days had some rough moments; once, the wind blew away their sheet music, distorted the sound, and the band was booed. Nevertheless, they continued playing together and eventually earned fame. The photograph is courtesy of the McArthur Library.

La Fanfare Painchaud got their first military uniforms in 1885. This picture shows them at City Square in their second set of uniforms, purchased in 1890 especially for a competition in Quebec. They won first prize by marching into the hall and up several flights of stairs without missing a note. The photograph is courtesy of the McArthur Library.

Joseph Martin was the longest-tenured director of Painchaud's band, leading it from 1910 to 1959. He was leader of the Old Orchard Pier Casino Band at the time he took charge. He joined Painchaud's band at the age of 17 and had a long career with them, leading the band through two world wars. The photograph is courtesy of the Biddeford Historical Society.

Painchaud's band became the official band of the Maine 1st Regiment. When it was called away from Biddeford in the Spanish-American War, the Biddeford National Band substituted for local needs. Roy Sherwood was president of the band. They are shown here at Camp Ellis in 1911. Pierre Painchaud died in 1909. The photograph is courtesy of the McArthur Library.

The Gilbert and Sullivan Company also did *The Mikado*. The Japanese lanterns, umbrellas, and fans on stage were Japan's best-known exports at the time. They were collected as Christmas ornaments or as lawn party ornaments. They are today prized collectors' items. The photograph is courtesy of the Biddeford Historical Society.

This is the stage of the Biddeford Opera House, set for a graduation in 1890. It had a large stage but low rigging. The floor was flat, and seating was by numbered bench. The hall was lost in 1894 to fire. The benches look new; the whole building had recently undergone a renewal, including the installation of a fire sprinkler system.

Pictured here is Biddeford City Hall on the morning of December 31, 1894, when it burned down to its first floor. Firemen thought they had things under control and did not engage the new sprinkler system because it would flood the whole building. The fire started from a cigar that burned through a wastebasket and then spread throughout the building. The photograph is courtesy of the McArthur Library.

72

Architect John Calvin Stevens was willing to work with the city, which was very much underinsured. He saved the granite façade of the first floor and produced a much better building in an eclectic style. The top of the tower from the clock up is wood painted the same color as the brick to save money. Additions to the rear of the building greatly enlarged it. The city was allotted much more space in the new building by some small additions to the rear. The utility of the building was vastly increased. The photograph is courtesy of the McArthur Library.

The new auditorium was tangent to the street and much larger. The second-floor lobby was kept, but the hilly lot was taken advantage of, and the auditorium had sloping floors and exits on the ground level. The photograph is courtesy of the McArthur Library.

The stage of the new opera house was narrow; box seats to the left and right were perhaps considered but not built. The rigging was high and versatile. In this picture, the auditorium is bright with white brocade paper, and the stage moldings are covered with gilt leaves. In later years, as a motion picture theater, it was painted and papered in dark maroon. The photograph is courtesy of the McArthur Library.

Downtown Biddeford was a busy place by day or night. These workers are waiting outside the factory at 1:45 for the end of the lunch-hour warning bell. Factory life revolved around the factory clock. Biddeford had the nickname "the City of Bells," as churches also joined in at noon or before services. The photograph is courtesy of the McArthur Library.

Henry Goshen photographed the interior of Leo Baigay's restaurant in 1916. The establishment was located at 19 Alfred Street. Many workers would take a meal in a place like this at lunch or between shifts. The side streets along Main Street were dotted with lunchrooms. The photograph is by Bijou Studio, courtesy of the McArthur Library.

Moses Webber was paymaster at the Laconia Mills. He left Biddeford to manage mills in New Hampshire but remembered the people of Biddeford in his will, leaving $40,000 to help establish a hospital in Biddeford. Robert McArthur assisted the effort, and the Webber Hospital was formed. The photograph is courtesy of the McArthur Library.

To build and assist the Webber Hospital, the Webber Hospital Auxiliary created and put on performances year after year. This is the cast of *Our Gypsies*, which ran four nights and raised $1,800 for the hospital. The auxiliary was very active in the late 1970s, raising money for the current hospital. The photograph is courtesy of the McArthur Library.

The first Moses Webber Hospital opened in a large rented house on Pool Street. This 1911 class of nurses was the last to graduate from the Pool Street building. The new facility would eventually locate a nurse's home next to the hospital. The photograph, courtesy of the McArthur Library, is from the R.H. Gay Collection.

The dreams and hard work paid off in 1912. The Moses Webber Hospital was a dream come true for many citizens. The lot was very large, and the ground was not yet landscaped. The exterior was neoclassical, in keeping with the fashion of the times. It was not Biddeford's first hospital. The Trull Hospital was available in 1906 but used homeopathic remedies. The photograph is courtesy of the McArthur Library.

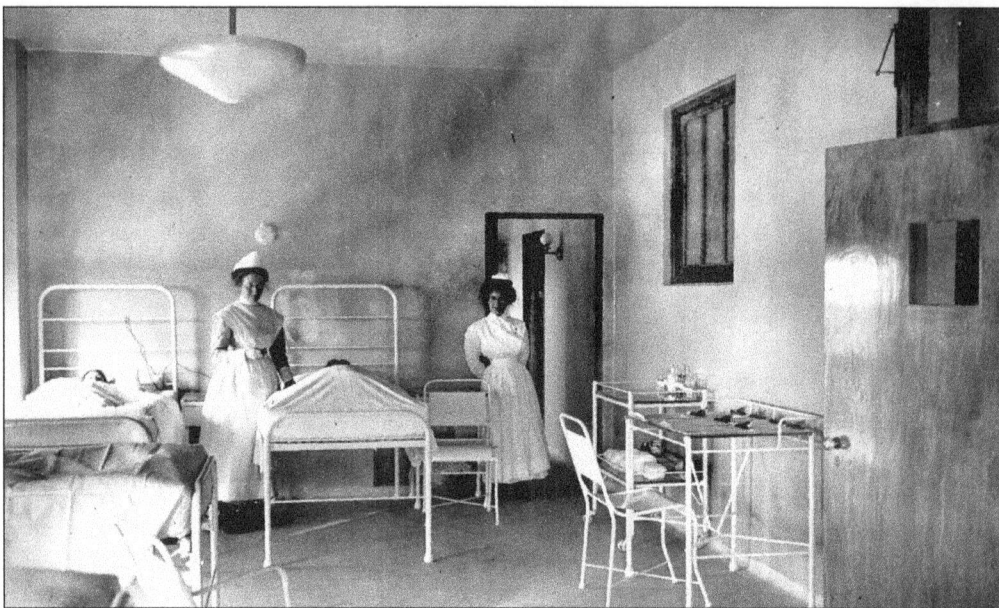

The wards in the new Webber Hospital must have seemed miraculous. Hard washable surfaces and sanitary metal furnishings were everywhere. The electric lighting was very modern for 1911. The modern rooms conflicted with the classical exterior. The photograph is from the R.H. Gay Collection, courtesy of the McArthur Library.

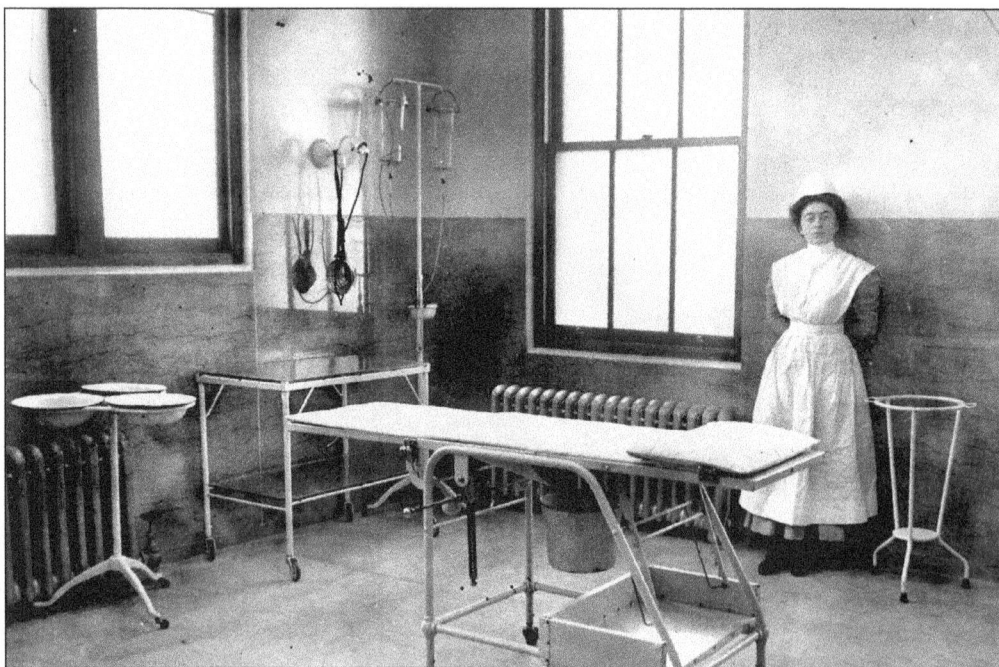

Shown is a surgery in the Webber Hospital in 1911. With its sparse equipment, it does not look modern by today's standards. The photograph, courtesy of the McArthur Library, is from the R.H. Gay Collection.

Six

FROM DOBBIN TO TIN LIZZIE

The horse and the ox moved the whole of New England society until the 19th and early 20th centuries. Then came the trains, planes, and automobiles. The change was relentless, steady, and profound.

Washington Street was dominated by the horse trade in the 19th century. These buildings were full of carriage makers, livery stables, and blacksmiths. Out of frame to the left is the City Central Fire Department. The central location was good for people in need of transportation, and it kept the most unsanitary part of 19th-century life in one place. The photograph is courtesy of the McArthur Library.

This is the Central Fire Station, built in 1907. It is shown here in 1940 with a mix of gasoline-powered equipment. The doors of the horse-drawn vehicle station could not accommodate modern fire equipment. As engines got bigger, it took more care to get them into the station. Eventually, rear-view mirrors had to be folded, and engines inched into place. The photograph is from the McArthur Library.

Two of Biddeford's steam pumps are shown here posing outside the Central Fire Station in 1908. The Fire Company was started in 1848 using the bell in the new high school as the town's fire bell. The *Richard Vines* (on the left) was bought in 1868. The *Eben Simpson* was purchased in 1869 and named after a past fire chief. The photograph is from the R.H. Gay Collection, courtesy of the McArthur Library.

Steamer No. 3 was purchased in May 1909. The power of the new engine was tested around the city and is shown here being tested at the Pepperell Mills. Also shown is the department's fuel wagon with a fresh load of firewood to keep the steamer steaming. The photograph is from the R.H. Gay Collection, courtesy of the McArthur Library.

This is the Biddeford department's hose wagon with a load of dried and folded hoses. Steam pumps were heavy with little cargo space and needed supply wagons. The stiff intake hoses were carried on the sides of the steam pumps, as they were needed first to get the pump set up. The photograph is from the author's collection.

The beveled-glass ports in the center lamp declare this is the *Eben Simpson* being proudly displayed outside the Central Fire Station *c.* 1922. Fire chief Charles Johnson would continue in 1923 the replacement of horse-drawn equipment. He chose the fire engine. The Ahrens-Fox could pump, move under power, carry its own hose and several firemen, and had special equipment like gas masks in individual fireproof boxes. The photograph is from the author's collection.

Biddeford fire chief Charles Bonser poses for Charles E. Moody in 1913. The fire chief needed a fast rig to get to the fire. The rig is polished like the engines, and the horse is so well groomed that he shines more than the rig. The photograph is courtesy of the McArthur Library.

The 1923 Ahrens-Fox is decorated for a parade in 1926. The pumping apparatus was in front of the engine. The large brass ball seemingly blocking the driver's view evened out the flow of the water with air pressure. On the running boards are fire extinguishers and other special equipment. The photograph is from an old postcard in the author's collection.

The Ahrens-Fox's capacity as a float in a parade allowed it to have a rescue scene on the back for the American Legion parade of November 1928. The firemen are Eugene Ricker, Chief Ernest Fournier, Lt. Edward Petit, Frank Cantara, Asst. Chief Edmund Pate, Fredric Lamirande, and Edmond Martin. On the engine are George Boisoeault, Ludger Lantagne, and Joseph Archambault. The photograph by Anastasoff is courtesy of the McArthur Library.

The Hamilton livery stable would park your horse for 10¢ a day or for 50¢ a week. The stable operated from 1880 to 1905. Workers could place their horse in Hamilton's care and be assured it was fed and watered. Guests at the Biddeford House could rent a horse and carriage and have greater freedom to move about the area. The photograph is courtesy of the McArthur Library.

Erwin S. Gowen's blacksmith shop was next to Hamilton's livery stable. They concentrated on farrier work, but there were wheel rims and carriage fittings to make. It was dangerous work despite devices to hold a horse steady. Every worker got kicked, some fatally. The photograph is courtesy of the McArthur Library, a gift of Harry W. Gowen.

The Townsend Brothers carriage shop was located at 9 Jefferson Street and operated from 1880 to 1910. The workers shown here include Fred Wayson, Charles H. Townsend, Jesse Charles Townsend, John Alden Townsend, George E. Townsend, and Alonzo Kimball. The photograph is courtesy of the McArthur Library, a gift of Ralph Watson.

Horsecars appeared on Biddeford streets in 1888. They were a short-lived sight because the line was converted to electric trolleys in 1892. The route reached from Five Points in Biddeford to town hall in Old Orchard. Eventually, connections could be made in Biddeford to the Atlantic Shore Line, or in Saco to the Portland Line. The photograph is courtesy of the McArthur Library.

This is Five Points in 1905. The trolley is rounding the turn to Elm Street. The country store selling pressed hay will become Ray Irving's garage. The trolley is a closed car used in cold or wet weather. Here we see three carriages, a safety bicycle, and a trolley, but no automobiles. They were available in 1905 but very scarce. The photograph is courtesy of the McArthur Library.

Nobody liked to ride a closed trolley in the summer. Open cars like this one waiting on Main Street were the backbone of the summer fleet. The metal grid was a man catcher to prevent people from sliding under the wheels in a crowd. Canvas curtains could be pulled down in a summer rain. The photograph is courtesy of the McArthur Library.

Biddeford had service from two electric lines. This view of City Square shows an Atlantic Shore Line trolley coming into City Square. The terminus of the line was city hall. The interurban trolleys had better seats and a baggage compartment. They were closed cars and ran at high speed once out of the city limits. The photograph is courtesy of the McArthur Library.

Ed Ward was the agent in the Biddeford-Saco area for Indian motorcycles. Motorcycles were more than recreation vehicles when first invented. Automobiles were expensive; tradesmen were fond of cycles with a sidecar. They filled the sidecar with tools, and the cycle made a replacement for the traditional tradesman's pushcart. The photograph is courtesy of the McArthur Library.

Walter Clark, at Five Points near the Irving garage, sold the Harley-Davison cycle. These cyclists are about to begin a journey to the White Mountains from his shop in 1917. For most of them, it will be the farthest they have ever been from Biddeford. Small mementos will be bought and kept for a lifetime. The photograph is from the author's collection.

When the stables started coming down on Washington Street, garages went up. This garage was one of three in Biddeford in 1915. The Dodge car is advertised for sale at $785. Most Biddeford residents would have to buy used cars, despite this low price by today's standards. The photograph is from the R.H. Gay Collection, courtesy of the McArthur Library.

If bad roads caused your car to break down, the Franklin Street Garage was one of the better places to gas up and repair your car in the 1920s. Franklin Street is very narrow; the gas pumps directly on the sidewalk would be a terrible hazard today. The building housed a bowling alley on the second floor. Bowling became popular in Biddeford in the 1830s and remained so into the 1950s. Many downtown buildings had bowling alleys in a corner or in the basement. The old garage has been removed for a parking lot. The photograph is courtesy of the McArthur Library.

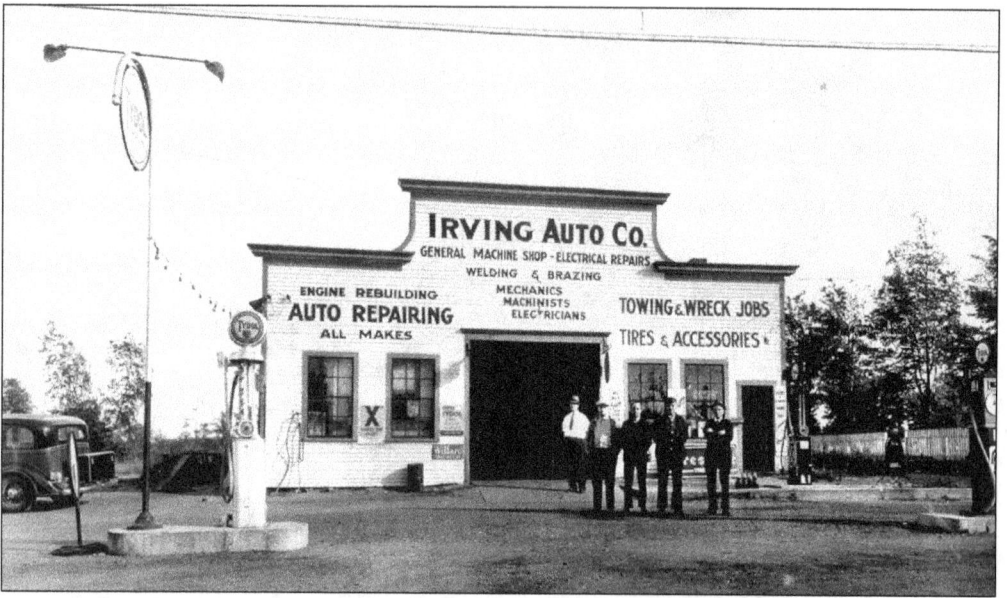

Ray Irving's garage, at Five Points, could provide any service a car might need—mechanical, electrical, or machine work. Ray, who owned a machine lathe as a teenager, went on to earn a degree in electrical engineering. The garage was destroyed by fire in World War II, when it was being used by troops on the coast as a motor pool. The photograph is courtesy of the McArthur Library.

Artist James Montgomery Flag, famous for his "I Want You" Uncle Sam poster, could afford a car. He is on the left in white pants. Notice that the car has two spares on the rack. Flag tried to embarrass the city into improving the Pool Road by publishing an illustrated poem in the local paper about the roughness of the road. The photograph is from the R.H. Gay Collection, courtesy of the McArthur Library.

The 1920 interior of the Franklin Street Garage displays a variety of automotive products. The radiators appear to be for Model Ts. The shellacked wainscoted interior was gloomy, but it was the standard for workplaces like railroad stations or fire stations. The photograph is courtesy of the McArthur Library.

The horse's place was challenged off the road in logging by machines like this early tracked vehicle. The stout wagon is Charles Johnson's and was being used in the stone quarries at the time. The weight is scrawled on the picture as 9,910 pounds. The scene is in front of the ABC building on Main Street. The photograph is from the author's collection.

The tercentenary of Richard Vines's landing was celebrated in 1916. This decorated car advocated women's right to vote. The suffragettes in the car are Mrs. David Dollif, Mrs. Harry W. Libby, Mrs. Martin Kingsbury, and Mrs. Anthony Fernans. Arthur Lemieux is driving. Only 35 cars were found in the city to decorate. The photograph is from the R.H. Gay Collection, courtesy of the McArthur Library.

One of the better-known drivers in Biddeford was Walter A. Gowen, a Civil War veteran. He was born in 1846 and enlisted in 1862. He served in the Maine 27th Regiment. A railroad man after the war, he became engineer of the Flying Yankee. The photograph was made in 1939. Gowen survived until 1941. The photograph is courtesy of the Biddeford Historical Society.

Seven

At the Beach
and on the River

The life of the waterman was less affected by the changes stirring in the factories. The economy of fuel and wage kept the sailing vessel alive for years. The biggest changes in Biddeford along the water came from people having leisure time and the wealth to use it in travel. Biddeford Pool became a destination to escape the summer city heat as well as a good small harbor to fish from.

The tug *Joseph Baker* is tied up in the gut at Biddeford Pool. The tug was a familiar sight along the river in the late 1800s; Charles E. Goldthwaite guided the vessel for years. The rocky landscape shows how much human landscaping has changed the appearance of the Pool. In an age when wood was cheap fuel, the Pool was treeless. The photograph is courtesy of the McArthur Library.

Saco River pilot Charles E. Goldthwaite is shown here relaxing on the stern of the *Joseph Baker*. Goldthwaite was born in 1851 and served 35 years on the Saco River. He died in 1907. He looks like the very stereotype of the self-confident sailor of the 1800s. The first Goldthwaite at Biddeford Pool was Captain Phillip, who married Mary Jordan in 1758. Phillip had the fortune or misfortune to be the king's revenue agent at the time of the Revolution and removed to Canada when serious assaults on officials began. The family returned. The photograph is courtesy of the McArthur Library, a gift of Mrs. C.R. Means.

The tugboat A.G. *Prentiss* was identifiable by the gold eagle on the wheelhouse. It was a most familiar sight on the Saco River. It was constantly handling river traffic between the ocean and the wharves at the falls. Locals Capt. Tristram Goldthwaite and fireman Edward Goulet manned her. The photograph is courtesy of the McArthur Library.

One of the favorite sights of people along the river was that of a coastal schooner being towed into Biddeford or out to sea. Schooner shipping persisted until World War II because the ships had low labor cost and remained competitive with steam. In this scene, the tug A.G. *Prentiss* is towing the schooner *Jeremiah Smith*. The photograph is from the R.H. Gay Collection, courtesy of the McArthur Library.

The crew of the A.G. *Prentiss* in 1916 included captain and pilot Clarence Goldthwaite (in the center) and engineer Frank B. Lockray (on the left). The Goldthwaites were descendants of Samuel Jordan, and they lived in the old trading post for generations. Some of them were well-known pilots on the Saco River. One other Tristram Goldthwaite also captained the A.G. *Prentiss* in the 1920s. The photograph is by Charles Moody, courtesy of the McArthur Library.

The A.G. *Prentiss* is towing the barge *Tonickon* of Philadelphia. The Pepperell Mills used 22,000 tons of coal a year. Most homes heated and cooked with coal. The gas and electric works ran on coal. The amount of coal was staggering. The ashes were used to fill in the clay pits dug to build the mills. The photograph is from the R.H. Gay Collection, courtesy of the McArthur Library.

Local transportation used the river instead of the roads. The Pool Road along the Saco River was notoriously bad. The side-wheel steamer *S.E. Spring* made the excursion from Factory Island to Camp Ellis and Biddeford Pool in the 1880s. It is shown here in the gut at Biddeford Pool. Colonel Cutts' old marine store can be seen behind the stern. The photograph is courtesy of the McArthur Library.

The little excursion boat *Item* was a source of tragedy in 1909. It headed out with a load of city people to view the *Sylph*, a yacht President Taft was using. The *Item* overturned when everyone rushed to one side as it approached the yacht. Two people were drowned. The photograph is from the R.H. Gay Collection, courtesy of the McArthur Library.

Known as Piper's boats, the *Goldenrod* and a sister ship, the *Nimrod*, offered a way to cool off on the river if one did not sit too close to the boiler or engine. Diversions at the end of the trip included dinner at a seashore restaurant, taking the Dummy Railroad to the amusements at Old Orchard, or an afternoon blueberry picking on the New Town Road. The photograph is courtesy of the McArthur Library.

War conditions in 1918 brightened the future of sailing. The old Perkins shipyard was reopened as the Biddeford Shipbuilding Company. They built the *Jere G. Shaw*. The *Shaw* was built with shares sold to local investors. It proved so unprofitable that it had to be sold at a loss. William H. Gould (the third man on the left in the second row) would captain the vessel. The photograph is courtesy of the McArthur Library.

The *Jere G. Shaw* is being towed out to sea. It was very expensive to build and was made of wartime oak lumber of extraordinary lengths. It was said that it was overbuilt, with enough lumber for two ships. Its sails were damaged on its first voyage south, and the extra bill to investors was $2,700. The photograph, a gift of Oscar Hanson, is courtesy of the McArthur Library.

The *Jere G. Shaw*, with pennants flying, is preparing for its maiden voyage. It looks a little out of place with the electric company's smokestack and towers in the background. The vessel was sold at a loss after being damaged in a storm. It sank in a great storm off Cape Hatteras in 1930. It weighed 739 tons and had a beam of 36 feet and a length of 193 feet. The photograph is courtesy of the McArthur Library.

Tourist business at Biddeford Pool began in 1833 with the Mansion House of Batchelder Hussy. The first guest came from Lowell in 1833. The Husseys were famous for their clam chowder. The photograph is courtesy of the McArthur Library, a gift of Harry W. Owen.

The store of G.H. Hussey, at Biddeford Pool, was the post office in 1896. Oren B. Edwards was the local express and mailman. He kept Biddeford Pool connected to the city at the falls through the mail and delivery of goods by express. The wagon and team belong to Edwards. The photograph is courtesy of the McArthur Library.

One of the grander hotels to develop at the Pool was the Ocean View, built by Thomas Evans. It is shown here reflected in the Great Pond at Biddeford Pool in 1909. It became Marie Joseph Academy and, later, the Marie Joseph Spiritual Center. The opposite face of the hotel is on an excellent beach. The photograph is from the R.H. Gay Collection, courtesy of the McArthur Library.

This is the Biddeford Pool herring fleet in 1883. Fish and lobsters were shipped to larger ports like Boston and Portland to get the best price. The commercial methods of lobster fishing were just developing. Many lobster-fishing methods were developed at Biddeford Pool. The photograph is courtesy of the McArthur Library.

Fishermen are at Biddeford Pool repairing their nets in 1917. The men are, from left to right, Irving S. Migrate, Charles Hatch, and Fred Waterhouse. Hatch and Waterhouse were partners for 40 years. They lived in their fishing shack. The photograph is from the R.H. Gay Collection, courtesy of the McArthur Library.

The Abinakee Club offered a golf course, a clubhouse, tennis courts, and a croquet court. It was a much more pleasant prospect than a few years before. Rich people from the Cincinnati area discovered the Pool and colonized it every summer. The photograph is from the R.H. Gay Collection, courtesy of the McArthur Library.

Stone Cliff, the cottage of the Tidd family, is one of the grander cottages near the Abinakee Club. It is a great example of the Shingle style, complete with porte-cochère and outbuildings for guest and servants. The photograph is from the R.H. Gay Collection, courtesy of the McArthur Library.

This cottage belonged to President Taft's niece. Her father built the cottage as his summer retreat from Cincinnati. The president visited several times by yacht and by car. The photograph is from the R.H. Gay Collection, courtesy of the McArthur Library.

President Taft is coming ashore at Biddeford Pool in 1910. The president's brother-in-law and niece summered at Biddeford Pool. The heavy president sank the floating dock and wet his feet. The surface of the platform is soaked. The man in white with a sword is Archie Butts, who would die on the *Titanic* in 1912. The photograph is from the R.H. Gay Collection, courtesy of the McArthur Library.

Eight

FAITHS AND FRIENDSHIPS

Biddeford accepted wave after wave of immigrants as the mills sought more labor from around the world. In 1830, political unrest in Biddeford sparked violence, but the development of fraternal organizations acted as a safety valve. These organizations provided a place—outside of church—where people of like cultures, values, and politics could gather with a purpose more noble than troublemaking.

The Freemasons developed in 1717; they spread from England to New England almost at once. Biddeford has had two Masonic lodges: the Palestine and the Dunlap. Members of the short-lived Palestine Lodge met in the Marble Hall. Those of Dunlap Lodge met in the Masonic building on Main Street. Built in 1895, it was the best business block in the city. The photograph is courtesy of the McArthur Library.

The oldest social group in Biddeford appears to be "the Ancient and Honorables." They claimed to have been founded in 1800. In this picture, they are having a clambake in Richard Vines's old barley field at Biddeford Pool in 1910. The newspapers mention their meetings nearly every summer in the late 1800s. The photograph is from the R.H. Gay Collection at the McArthur Library.

Stereographer B.F. Cole captured the Odd Fellows building in 1873 before it was doubled in size. For years, they swapped dedication and groundbreaking honors with the Masons as the city continued to grow. The Knights of Labor used the Odd Fellows hall as an early meeting place as trade unions were trying to become established. The photograph is courtesy of the McArthur Library, a gift of Mrs. Raymond Means.

This is a Labor Day parade from 1907. Labor organization was starting to take root. It faced corporate, government, and church hostility. Roman Catholics were threatened with excommunication if they joined a union. The most crippling strike occurred in 1916. The photograph is courtesy of the McArthur Library.

Football was a different sport when everyone played instead of watching. This is the Biddeford High School team of 1893. High school sports followed the example of college sports and formed teams to play other schools. The uniforms must have been very hot, as they were quilted like football uniforms of the times. The photograph is courtesy of the McArthur Library.

Baseball enjoyed rapid growth after the Civil War, and many local teams were formed. Factories sponsored teams, schools sponsored teams, churches sponsored teams, and teams formed among neighborhood friends. The Diamond Match Company had a large sash and door factory and lumberyard in Biddeford. This is the Diamond team in 1916. The photograph is from the R.H. Gay Collection, courtesy of the McArthur Library.

The curriculum at Biddeford High School included rifle corps training. This photograph, taken by N.P. Renout, shows the corps on the lawn of the school in 1891. The uniforms are cadet gray and reminiscent of the Civil War. The photograph is courtesy of the Biddeford Historical Society.

The ladies at Biddeford High School were not outdone. They had dark-blue uniforms. The drummers had jackets with embroidered frogs, similar to Civil War Zouauve jackets. The officers have sabers, but the ladies do not carry rifles. The photograph is courtesy of the McArthur Library.

St. Andre's School had a cadet corps as well. Today, the sight of youngsters carrying bayoneted rifles would seem strange. At one time, however, they were popular in schools (both public and private) and were often associated with churches. This group of cadets is posing on the steps of St. Andre's Church. The photograph is courtesy of the McArthur Library.

The Knights Templer is marching on upper Main Street. The Masons, Knights of Columbus, Odd Fellows, and Knights of Pythias all frequently marched. Every parade had a sense of suspense until your group or family member was seen to pass. The photograph is from the R.H. Gay Collection, courtesy of the McArthur Library.

The St. John Baptiste de Bienfaissance is a Franco-American group organized in 1867. Dr. Thivierge bought this building. It is decorated for St. John's Day, June 24, 1875. In 1896, the society constructed a building on Main Street to rival the Masonic building. The photograph, a gift of Raoul Labranche, is from the McArthur Library.

St. Mary's School, Biddeford, Me.

The Irish Catholics met in the Pepperell Counting House in 1850. They soon had an impressive complex occupying one side of St. Mary's Street. The first church was built in 1856. Francis Fassett designed the school in 1892. It completed a set of buildings along the street. Only one original building remains. The photograph is from a church brochure, courtesy of the McArthur Library.

Universalists built this church on City Square in 1867. The concept was slow to be accepted in Biddeford, and the church was weak in the 1950s. The Universalists now meet with the Unitarians in Saco. The Second Parish Congregational Church's first steeple can be seen in the background. The photograph is courtesy of the McArthur Library.

Franco-Americans made their intentions to stay known through the most dramatic of Biddeford's churches, St. Joseph's Roman Catholic Church, built in 1873–1883 in the city center. Its steeple can be seen from the city limits. The largest influx of French Canadians began in 1870. Successful western farms made farming in the East difficult in both Canada and the United States. The parish was founded in 1870. The French found it difficult to worship with the Irish and longed for a church like their own in Canada. The photograph is courtesy of the McArthur Library.

The Christ's Episcopal Church congregation was mostly workers from England in the Saco Water Power Company machine shop. They built this building on Bacon Street in 1874. They sold it in 1906 after building a more traditional structure in brick on Cresent Street. It became Etz Chaim Synagogue in 1906. The bell tower has been removed. The photograph is from the R.H. Gay Collection, courtesy of the McArthur Library.

The Methodists built this church on Foss Street in 1870 to replace the Alfred Street church. It had grown too small. The corner of Pool and Foss was called Amen Corner. It was the highest place in Biddeford until 1949, when lightning caused a fire in the steeple. The photograph is courtesy of the McArthur Library.

St. Andre's Roman Catholic Church made Biddeford a three-parish city. The French-speaking population clustered around the mills. When triple-deckers went up around the heights, a second parish was established in the center. It is shown under construction in 1909–1910. The photograph is from the R.H. Gay Collection, courtesy of the McArthur Library.

R.H. Gay photographed the interior of St. Andre's as the church neared dedication in 1910. St. Andre's also had a grammar school, which opened in 1900. The church took a decade to build. The finished building was not as ornamented as the original plans had indicated. The photograph is from the R.H. Gay Collection, courtesy of the McArthur Library.

114

Biddeford's Orthodox community worshiped in this building at the end of Emery Street from 1908 to 1936. They then purchased the Free Will Baptist Church on Adams Street and remodeled it in the 1950s. Other southern Mediterranean immigrants were Italians, Albanians, and Turks. Special interest has recently been shown in the Albanians and Turks, who are thought to have established a mosque meeting in the old Pepperell Counting House. It was possibly the site of the first mosque in the nation. The photograph is courtesy of the McArthur Library.

Greeks worked in the mills and the stone quarries. Shown here is the interior of the Greek Orthodox church on Emery Street near Main Street. The photograph was made c. 1918. The old practice of standing during worship was followed. The gentleman on the right is Savas Savidis, a teacher of Greek. The photograph is by Anastasoff and is courtesy of the McArthur Library.

On March 19, 1917, the ladies' Sunday school class of the United Baptist Church poses in costume for a St. Patrick's Day social on Jefferson Street in Biddeford. The church was originally the Cedar Street Baptist Church. The Baptist congregation was very active in the early 20th century. Reverend Morrison, in the rear right, guided the congregation at the time. The photograph is from the author's collection.

116

Nine

WAR AND DEPRESSION

Nineteen eighteen was a watershed year. American textile production leveled off when Japan separated the United States from the Asian market. Southern mills took over more and more U.S. production, leading to the end of New England's industrial heyday. After 1928, the mills resorted to short weeks in an attempt to retain experienced workers. By 1940, the city of Biddeford was bankrupt and in debt.

During the period that the Tattersons occupied the old Jordan house, it became something of a cultural icon, a rival to Quillcote in Buxton. The house was enlarged, and a porte-cochère was added. The hillside lot sported a tall flagpole. The house hosted weddings, parties, and plays on the lawn. A *Midsummer Night's Dream* was popular. The photograph is courtesy of the Biddeford Historical Society.

Colonial Revival was an accepted turn-of-the-century style, but there was little that was revivalist in the Jordan house parlor. The Governor Winthrop–style desk was original to the house. The rooms featured corner cupboards and pocket shuttered windows. The photograph is from the R.H. Gay Collection, courtesy of the McArthur Library.

When war was declared on Germany, the residents of Biddeford Pool organized a refined way to raise funds for charity. An elegant lawn party was held at the Foster residence. The lawn opened onto the links of the Abenakee Golf Course. Amusements included pony cart rides for the youngsters. The photograph is from the R.H. Gay Collection, courtesy of the McArthur Library.

118

The elegantly dressed party guests at the War Relief Lawn Party gather on the porch of the Foster house. Amenities such as the boy selling cigarettes helped raise funds for charity. The photograph is from the R.H. Gay Collection, courtesy of the McArthur Library.

Artist Ashton Knight painted for charity at the War Relief Lawn Party. He was a resident at Biddeford Pool and the son of expatriate American artist parents in Paris. His umbrella advertises Bloomingdale's as New York's greatest department store, reached by easy trolley transfers. The photograph is from the R.H. Gay Collection, courtesy of the McArthur Library.

When war was declared on Germany on April 6, 1917, it was decided that the city should support the effort with Flag Raising Day, held on April 14. Fourteen 10- by 15-foot flags were raised in different parts of the city. The first was on Alfred Street in front of the Odd Fellows hall. The photograph is from the R.H. Gay Collection, courtesy of the McArthur Library.

The flag raised on April 14, 1917, weighed 300 pounds and was borrowed from the Filene's department store in Boston. A crew on the roof lowered it over the front of the Lincoln Street Mill. The huge flag covered about a quarter of the front of the eight-million-square-foot building. The photograph is from the R.H. Gay Collection, courtesy of the McArthur Library.

120

In this July 1917 photograph, the faces of the men following the troops as the 7th Coastal Artillery marches around Biddeford and Saco tell of somber emotions. The photograph is from the R.H. Gay Collection, courtesy of the McArthur Library.

The Maine 7th Coastal Artillery came to Biddeford for the special flag-rising day. They marched around to sites, acting as an honor guard by hanging giant flags. The citizens are gathering in City Square to watch the unfurling of a giant flag on the front of the Pepperell Mills. The photograph is from the R.H. Gay Collection, courtesy of the McArthur Library.

Robert Hunter stands beside the Swift & Company delivery truck. By 1920, companies like Swift and Armor in the Midwest made huge profits on by-products and sold beef at prices that excluded Maine farmers from the market. Agriculture was disappearing as part of the Biddeford economy. The photograph is part of the author's collection.

The Johnson and Staples boatyard expanded to family property on Church Point. Orders of motor yachts like this one halted with the crash of 1929. The yard continued as the Marblehead Boat Yard. Some Johnson and Staples boats are still in service in New York City and Florida. The photograph is courtesy of the Biddeford Historical Society.

Workers in the Pepperell cloth hall gather for a photograph for the *Pepperell Sheet*. The woman second from the right in front is the author's grandmother Elsie Butler. Because of short time, her income fell to $6.50 a week. She left the mill after finding other employment. It was a difficult choice to make; workers faced blacklists. The photograph is from the author's collection.

Weather across the nation took a turn for the worse in the 1920s. This wrecked cottage at Hills Beach in Biddeford helped convince engineers to lengthen the breakwater at Camp Ellis. People envisioned a total washout of Hills Beach. The photograph is from the author's collection.

December 18–19, 1929, brought a major challenge to the power company. It was 28 degrees, and it rained for two days. This Johnson family photograph was taken on December 20. The scene is Meetinghouse Road. General, the family dog, is bewildered by the situation. The ice was so bad that horses could not stand if faced with a grade. The photograph is from the author's collection.

The cement ruins of distribution towers in the Saco River and along the shore puzzle people today. Linemen facing the storm of 1929 were told to expect 15 pounds of ice per foot of wire if conditions persisted. When it was over, the transmission towers looked like those in this photograph, with York Heat and Light in the background. The photograph is from the R.H. Gay Collection, courtesy of the McArthur Library.

In 1928, storms convinced everyone that the breakwater at Camp Ellis needed extending. Retired fire chief Charles Johnson hired out his team and stout wagon to move the stone to the quarry dock on Pool Street. He had retired to a farm on Meetinghouse Road. Johnson is shown with his hands on his hips. The photograph is from the author's collection.

After years of disuse and the 1947 forest fire, nothing now remains of Andrew's quarry but the pit and some rusting iron fittings. The quarry was opened for the rebuilding of the Camp Ellis breakwater in 1928. This photograph shows the old derricks in use. They were hand-wound and hand-swung, with men standing respectfully away from the stone. The photograph is from the author's collection.

This three-masted schooner is at the quarry dock on the Saco River. Thousands of tons of Biddeford granite were shipped from here. Projects like the Brooklyn Bridge, Boston Harbor's docks, and local breakwaters used Biddeford granite. The photograph is from the R.H. Gay Collection, courtesy of the McArthur Library.

For tradesman out of work in the winter, part-time work could be found in the ice industry. The team of horses is pulling a groover, a plowlike saw that scored the ice for splitting into sections. The teams wore calked shoes to avoid slipping. This scene is c. 1912, as ice cutting developed late in Biddeford. The photograph, by Charles Moody, is courtesy of the McArthur Library.

After the groover did its job, the ice was crosscut with an ice saw. The saw resembled a logger's whipsaw, except the handle was at a right angle to the blade. Men wore high calked logging boots on the ice to avoid falls. The photograph is by Charles Moody, courtesy of the McArthur Library.

Ice was moved into the icehouse by a conveyer. The ice was stored several stories high within the insulated building. The scene is likely at Pelletier's Ice House. The photograph is by Charles Moody, courtesy of the McArthur Library.

Local contractors were quick to take the job when Vito Mininni, a local masonry contractor, wanted this small stucco cottage at Hills Beach. Jobs for tradesmen were all but nonexistent, and Mininni could name whoever he wanted to do the work. The photograph is from the author's collection.

With poor soil and increasing western competition, Maine farmers concentrated on specialty crops. The Guinea Road area in Biddeford was devoted to strawberries. These pickers on the George Robbins farm likely got ½¢ per box. More than one 1930s radio was bought a half cent at a time. The photograph is courtesy of the McArthur Library.

www.ingramcontent.com/pod-product-compliance
Lightning Source LLC
Chambersburg PA
CBHW080559110426
42813CB00006B/1346